Turning Points

Program Authors

Connie Juel, Ph.D.

Jeanne R. Paratore, Ed.D.

Deborah Simmons, Ph.D.

Sharon Vaughn, Ph.D.

W9-BNU-466

PEARSON
Scott
Foresman

Glenview, Illinois
Boston, Massachusetts
Chandler, Arizona
Upper Saddle River, New Jersey

ISBN-13: 978-0-328-45286-6
ISBN-10:   0-328-45286-6

10 V011 14
CC1

Turning Points

Diversity

Contents

Diversity

Words 2 the Wise

Diversity is all about different kinds of people. This week you'll explore how different people connect with each other. As you read, think about the diversity around you.

Diversity

Look at a calendar. Somewhere on this date, people might be enjoying a special day. It might be the Chinese New Year. A train of dragons weaves through the crowd. Lions dance in city streets. The Chinese have a different calendar from ours. Their New Year falls on a different day each year.

A dragon dance is part of a Chinese New Year celebration.

Maybe it is Cinco de Mayo. *Cinco de Mayo* means "the Fifth of May." Mexicans celebrate their 1862 victory over French soldiers. Many Mexican Americans celebrate this day too. They celebrate with parades, music, and food. It is part of their heritage.

On June 19th many African Americans observe Juneteenth. This day celebrates the end of slavery. Parades, games, and family parties make the day a happy one.

Music fills the air during Cinco de Mayo.

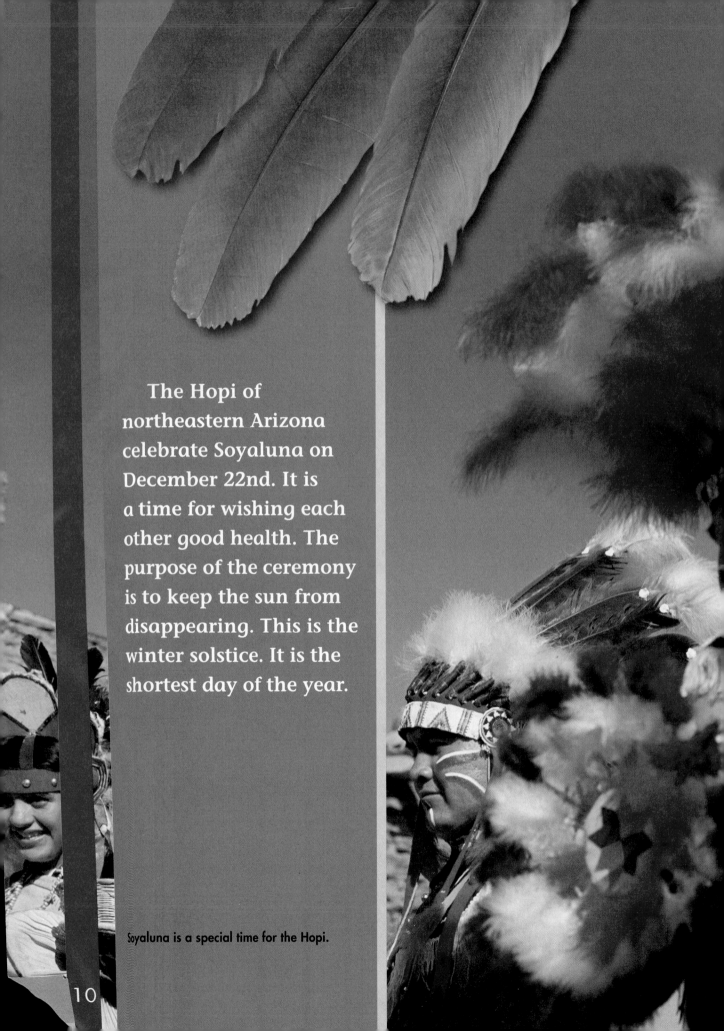

The Hopi of northeastern Arizona celebrate Soyaluna on December 22nd. It is a time for wishing each other good health. The purpose of the ceremony is to keep the sun from disappearing. This is the winter solstice. It is the shortest day of the year.

Soyaluna is a special time for the Hopi.

Many places also hold cultural festivals. This is when groups of people celebrate their ethnic roots. Going to a cultural festival is a great way to learn about another culture. Taste the food. Listen to the music. See the traditional clothing. Talk to people. It is fun!

The calendar is full of special days. These days show the wonderful diversity of our country. Celebrate!

Holidays bring people of all backgrounds together.

Beautiful Music

by Antonio Ortez

Have you ever heard of the Pied Piper? He played a musical instrument in Germany. Children followed its sound. What did he play? It was a flute. It didn't look like today's flutes. But it worked very much the same way.

Flutes have been part of German culture for hundreds of years. A German musician invented the modern flute in 1847.

Children loved the sound of the Pied Piper's instrument.

Flutes have been around for a long time. Scientists think the flute is over 50,000 years old! How do we know? Scientists found a bone fossil in France. Someone had made a flute from that bone. The fossil helped our understanding of that culture.

Many ethnic groups play instruments. The flute is one of the most popular. Would you like to learn how to play a flute? It's easy. You can practice with a soda bottle.

Right: Some of the first flutes were made from fossil bones.

Far right: This is a modern flute used in an orchestra.

First, keep your lips firm and your cheeks flat.
Second, place your lower lip against the edge of the
bottle's opening. Then, softly blow a steady stream of
air across the opening. You may have to move the bottle
until you hear a whistling sound. Can you hear it?
This is how a musician blows into a flute.

Blowing across bottles
makes sounds like a flute.

This girl is learning how
to play a recorder, a
type of flute.

There are many kinds of flutes. One type of flute is a kaval (kuh-VALL).

A kaval is made of hollow wood with holes in it. A player does not hold a kaval to the side. A player holds it out in front.

Shepherds have used kavals for thousands of years. They played them to lead sheep to pastures. People also played kavals for entertainment.

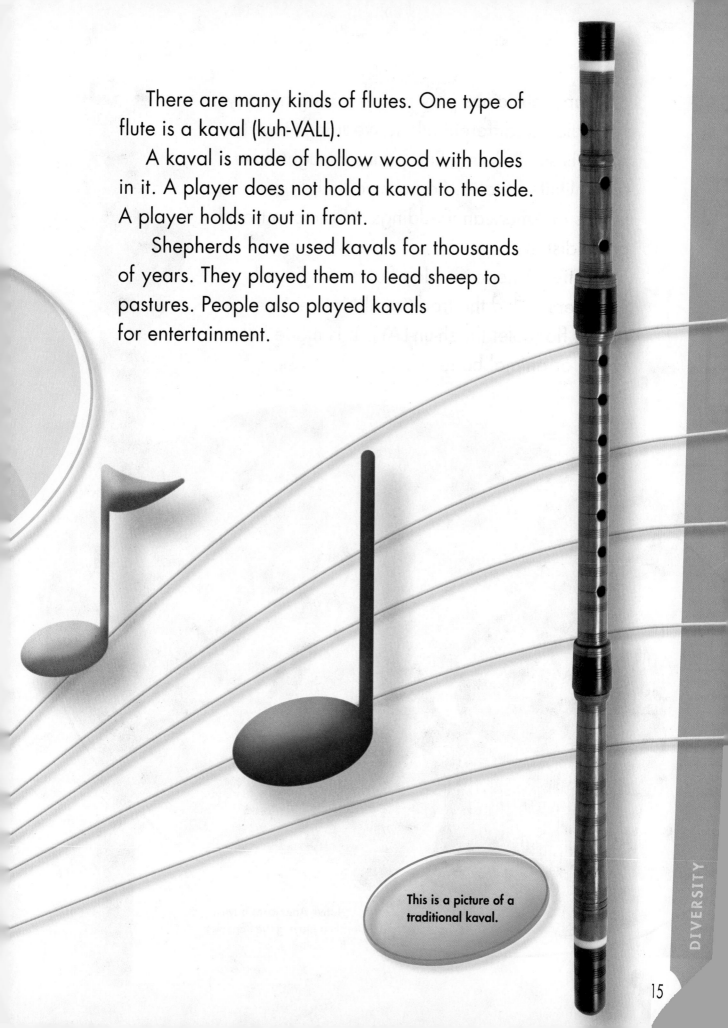

This is a picture of a traditional kaval.

Many musicians play kavals during holidays. They play at different ethnic weddings too. The kaval is small. Many Europeans brought them to the United States. So now you might even hear kavals at American weddings. Music can travel great distances.

Native Americans play flutes too. French explorers called the traditional Native American flute a flageolet (flazh-uh-LAY). It is made from wood or animal bone.

Native Americans have been playing the flageolet for centuries.

Native Americans used flageolets in many ceremonies. If a young man were dating a young woman, he could send her secret messages with flageolet music.

A tambin (tam-BIN) is a flute from Africa. It is made from a vine. It often is decorated with colored paper, tape, leather, or shells. The tambin is not well known. Some bands in the United States now feature this flute. Many people love listening to it. It creates a unique sound.

The tambin is becoming more popular in the United States.

Irish people have played wood-whistle flutes for centuries. But Robert Clarke made the first tin whistle in England in 1843. It became very popular in Ireland.

Clarke knew wooden flutes well. That understanding helped him make a tin one. First, he drilled six holes into a tin tube. Next, he cut a slit into a bit of wood. He shoved the wood into one end of the tube. Then Clarke blew through the slit and made music!

Clarke's company still makes tin whistles like this one.

The quena (KAY-nuh) looks a bit like a kaval. People from the Andes Mountains make quenas from wood. They have been doing this for thousands of years. They still play them today.

Think of all these different flutes. What would a band with all of them sound like? It might make special music. It might be like the Pied Piper's music. Flutes are like people. Together they make beautiful music!

kaval **tambin** **quena** **flageolet**

Kinds of Flutes

What Do You Think?

What steps must a person take to make an Irish tin whistle?

PAPER BIRDS
AND PLANTAINS

BY ELAINE A. KULE   ILLUSTRATED BY LAURIE KELLER

Last week my teacher, Ms. Abbot, told us about a new class project. She called it "Be a Teacher." Two students teach each other something about their cultures. Then, they teach what they have learned to the whole class. Ms. Abbot said it would give us a better understanding of other cultures. Miguel wanted Ms. Abbot to pair him with his best friend, Eddie.

Ms. Abbot read the list of student pairs. She said, "The last student pair is Miguel and Emi." Emi—that's me. Miguel groaned aloud.

"What is she going to teach me?" he asked loudly. "She doesn't even speak English!"

Ms. Abbot stared hard at Miguel.

"Miguel, I think this project has a lot to teach you," she said.

21

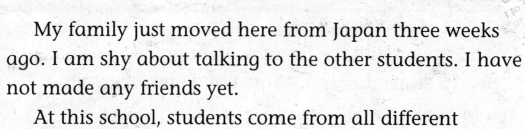

My family just moved here from Japan three weeks ago. I am shy about talking to the other students. I have not made any friends yet.

At this school, students come from all different backgrounds. I wanted to meet them. But I didn't feel comfortable speaking English. I learned some English in Japan. But, there are still so many words I don't know. My mother says I am just homesick. She says I should "be patient."

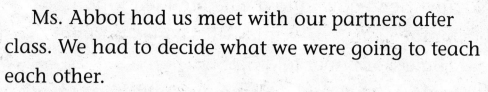

Ms. Abbot had us meet with our partners after class. We had to decide what we were going to teach each other.

Miguel walked slowly over to my desk. His head was down. "I guess we're working together," Miguel mumbled.

I nodded. Miguel pulled over an empty chair. He was staring at the paper bird I keep on my desk. I took the bird and placed it in his hand.

"Did you make this?" he asked. "It's great!"

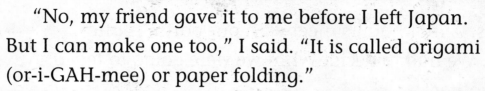

"No, my friend gave it to me before I left Japan. But I can make one too," I said. "It is called origami (or-i-GAH-mee) or paper folding."

"It's cool," Miguel said. "Hey, your English isn't bad at all. Why don't you ever talk?"

I shrugged. "I guess I don't have much to say," I answered.

"I have an idea!" Miguel said. "Why don't you teach me how to make a paper bird?"

"That's easy," I said. "And how about you? What can you teach me from your culture?"

"*Plantains con crema* (plahn-TAYNS kohn KRAY-muh) is my favorite dessert," Miguel said. "Plantains look like bananas."

Miguel came to my house for his origami lesson. I folded the paper step-by-step. He watched and practiced. He learned quickly.

The next day, I went to Miguel's house. He and his mom showed me how to make plantains.

Miguel translated into English what his mother said in Spanish.

First, we combined vanilla, cinnamon, and brown sugar and poured it over plantains. Then we baked the plantains.

Later, Miguel poured the *crema,* or cream, on them. "This is delicious," I said.

"Do you get homesick for Japan?" Miguel asked suddenly.

"Sometimes," I said.

"My mother misses Mexico," Miguel said. "I have to translate for her."

The presentations were the next week. Miguel and I shared what we learned with the class. He made a paper bird. I made a Mexican dessert. Everyone clapped.

So that is how my life changed. Many of the students wanted to make paper birds. We all had fun making them.

Miguel and I became friends too. He told Ms. Abbot that he had two new understandings. One was about origami. The other was about me.

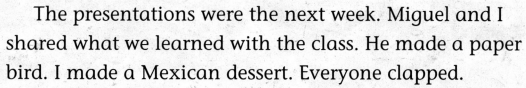

WHAT DO YOU THINK?

How did Miguel get to know Emi better?
What happened first, next, and last?

The residents of Metro Condos are having their monthly community dinner. Here is what's on the menu tonight.

The Garza family just moved into Metro Condos. This is their first community dinner. The whole family is cooking up a big pot of *sopa de pollo,* the most delicious chicken soup!

Mrs. O'Driscoll is bringing Limerick ham. It's made with berries and country-style mustard.

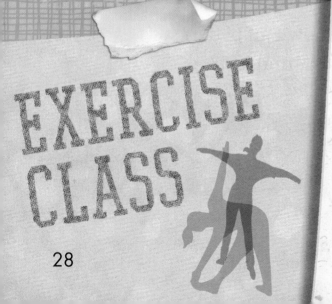

EXERCISE CLASS

What's for

The Garza Family's sopa de pollo
(Welcome to Metro Condos, Garzas!)

Mrs. O'Driscoll's Limerick ham

28

Supper?

The Hollisters' okra and shrimp

Mr. Hasim Ali's eggplant pancakes

Nikki and Albert Hollister made okra with shrimp tonight. The Hollisters hope the Garzas will like it.

Mr. Hasim Ali also wants to impress the Garzas. He made eggplant pancakes. This wonderful dish has cinnamon in it!

The Lo family will bring a Cambodian treat: a basket of sweet and sour chicken wings.

Other families in other condos are making tasty dishes too. What would you make?

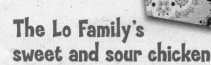

The Lo Family's sweet and sour chicken

DIVERSITY

4 YOU 2 DO

Word Play

Is it hard to learn a new language? Try this one. In this new language, the English alphabet is reversed. The letter *z* stands for *a*, *y* stands for *b*, and so on. Translate these two words from the new language into English.

vgsmrx   **xfogfiv**

Write this week's concept words in code.

Making Connections

You read about differences in flutes, food, and people's hobbies. Which did you know about before? Which would you like to learn more about or try? Tell why it is interesting to you.

On Paper

People from many lands have moved to the United States. If you moved to another country, what American traditions would you bring with you?

 Answers for Word Play: ethnic, culture

EXPLORATION

Contents

EXPLORATION

Words 2 the Wise

This week's concept is **exploration.** We will explore how we are able to see things both small and far. As you read, think about how far exploration can take us.

Let's Explore

ENDLESS DISCOVERIES

Many people think there is nothing left to discover. Those people are wrong. There is always a piece of land to explore. There is always a sea creature to learn about. And there is always a new star to discover.

Humans are curious. We learn when we explore. Sometimes we find things we are not looking for. And then we learn something new! Today, powerful telescopes and spacecraft take us farther into the universe. They help us learn about other planets. And they help us understand how big other galaxies are.

This is a picture from the Hubble telescope.
Inside these gas pillars stars could be forming.

35

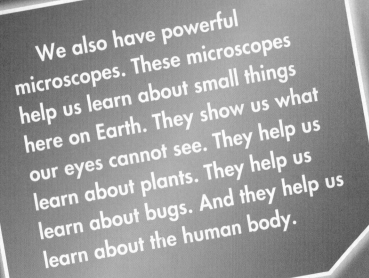

We also have powerful microscopes. These microscopes help us learn about small things here on Earth. They show us what our eyes cannot see. They help us learn about plants. They help us learn about bugs. And they help us learn about the human body.

This scientist is using an electron microscope.

There will always be something to explore. And there will always be more to learn. Curious people will try to solve the mysteries of the universe. And they will try to solve the mysteries here on Earth. We will always make new discoveries if we look close enough.

There is an old movie called *Fantastic Voyage*. Explorers in the movie shrink their bodies. They climb into a tiny submarine. The submarine travels into a strange territory. It travels inside a human body! The pioneers visit the heart of a living man. They also visit his brain.

The pioneers discover a problem in the man's body. They save his life.

Fantastic Voyage seemed amazing when it came out. Doctors today really can travel through the human body. But they do not shrink. They do not use tiny submarines. They use tiny cameras instead.

Old and New Ways

Imagine you have a serious stomach problem. How would doctors discover the cause? Forty years ago, doctors would X-ray your stomach. Then they might perform surgery to fix the problem.

The explorers in this movie are traveling inside a human body.

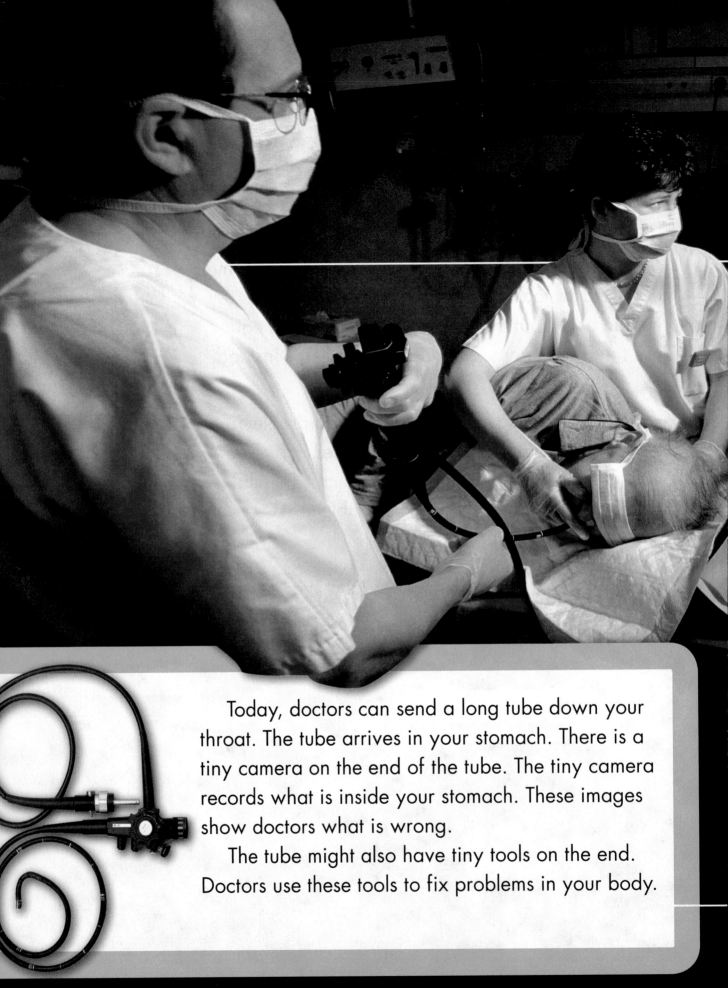

Today, doctors can send a long tube down your throat. The tube arrives in your stomach. There is a tiny camera on the end of the tube. The tiny camera records what is inside your stomach. These images show doctors what is wrong.

The tube might also have tiny tools on the end. Doctors use these tools to fix problems in your body.

The tube travels all the way to your stomach.

A Camera Pill

Now doctors have an even smaller camera. This camera is the size of a pill. You swallow it. The camera travels through the body. It sees the throat. It sees inside your stomach. It takes pictures of everything!

The pill travels where the tube cannot. And you will not feel the pill at all.

Which would you rather swallow, the tube or the pill?

Soon the camera's voyage is over. Doctors have lots of pictures of the inside of your body. They study the pictures. Then they try to find where the problem is.

Scientists hope to improve this camera. They want to put tiny tools on the pill. Doctors will move the tools by using remote controls. The pill will be more than a camera. It will also be a small robot.

These photos were taken by a camera pill.

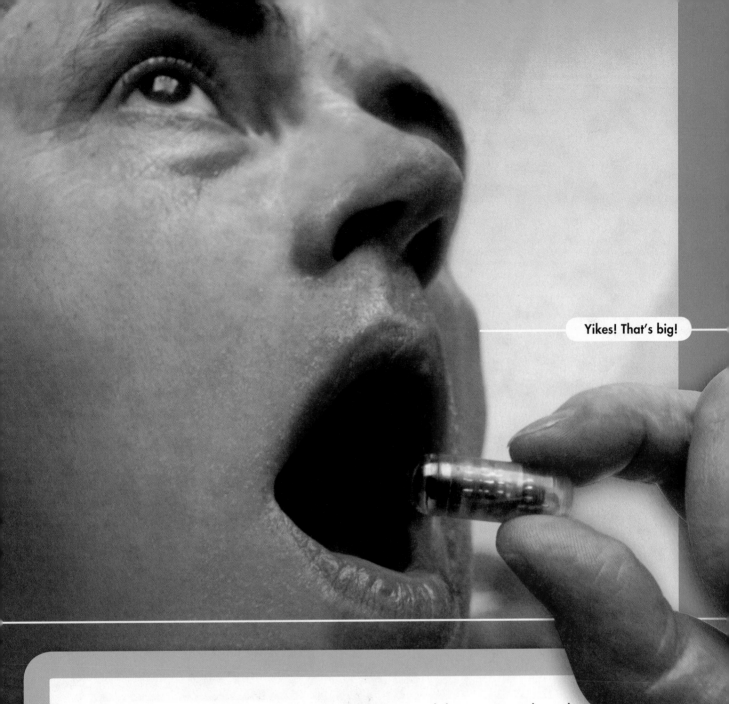

Yikes! That's big!

The camera pill is cool. But it has problems. It is hard to swallow. It is the size of a large jellybean. Scientists hope to make the pill smaller.

Also, the camera cannot reach all of the territories in the body. Scientists are working on that too. They made a new device with a different camera. It moves into remote places in the body.

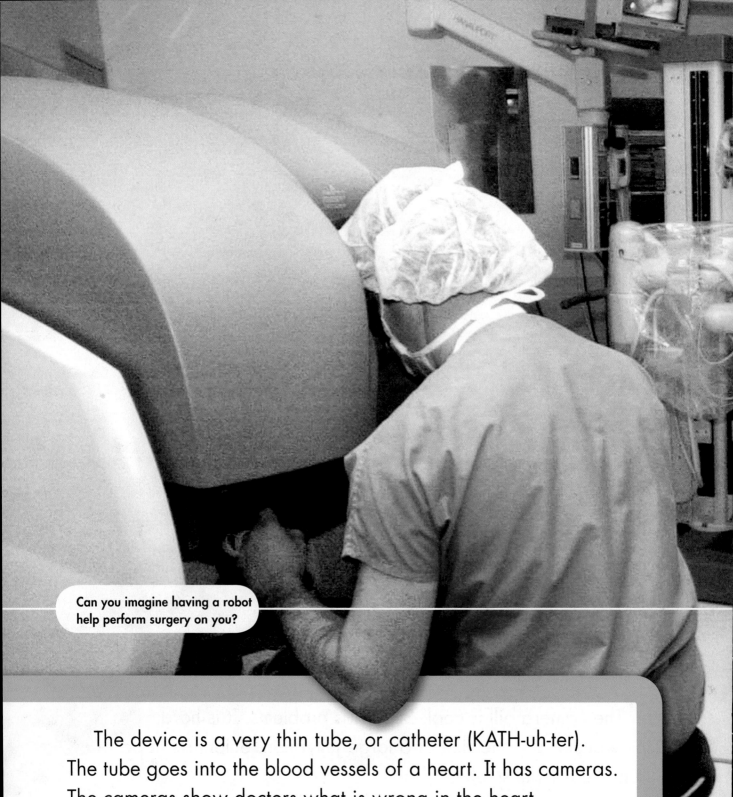

Can you imagine having a robot help perform surgery on you?

The device is a very thin tube, or catheter (KATH-uh-ter). The tube goes into the blood vessels of a heart. It has cameras. The cameras show doctors what is wrong in the heart.

Doctors have already used this device when they operate. They use it to fix problems in the heart. This new device helps doctors make fewer mistakes. It lets doctors operate on a heart in forty minutes or less.

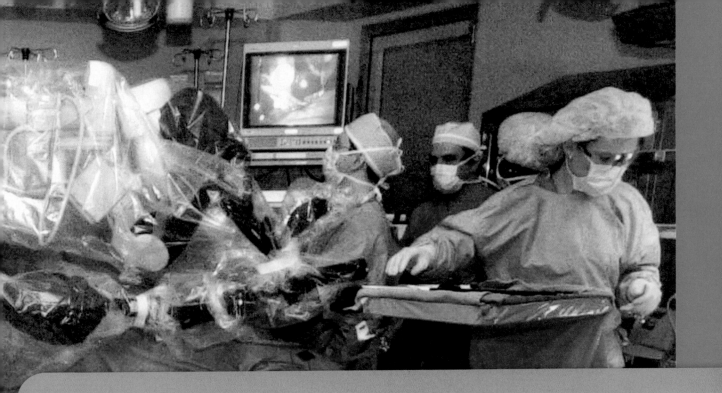

Devices such as the tube with cameras can also be part of a large robot. The robot helps doctors when they operate. It places the camera and the tube in the correct spot.

Doctors may never shrink themselves to explore the human body. But they are like the explorers in *Fantastic Voyage* in a way. They use small cameras. They use small tools. And they have a better understanding of the human body.

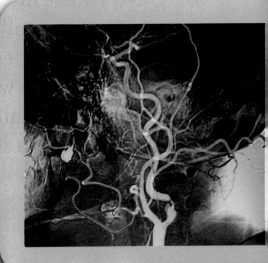

With a catheter, doctors can work their way through a patient's arteries.

What Do You Think?

If you were a doctor, how could small cameras help you?

DANGER
in the
Meadow

by Patricia Curtis Pfitsch

Belle's antennae trembled. She was dreaming of a monster with a loud growl.

When Belle opened her eyes, she realized she was on her sunflower. But she could still hear the terrible growling sound.

Everywhere insects were flying. "Get away as fast as you can!" they yelled.

Belle saw a green monster mowing down the meadow! She was confused. Jack the bee landed on her sunflower. "The meadow is under attack!" he shouted.

"The queen sent the worker bees to find a new home. Are you moving?" Jack asked curiously.

"Where will I go?" Belle wailed. "I'll be homesick if I leave."

"We can find a new home together," Jack said.

Belle stared at him. "Ladybugs and bees can't be friends!"

Jack laughed. "When troubles come, you make new friends."

Jack flew away. Belle saw the mysterious monster approaching, so she left.

GRRRR

Belle landed on a yellow mountain.

"This is a mysterious mountain," she said. She heard a buzzing sound. Jack had arrived.

"This will make a good home for the bees," he said.

"Bees and ladybugs can't be friends," Belle said. The mountain moved and Belle flew away.

"Jack!" she shouted. "Fly away fast!"

The mountain moved again. They escaped just in time.

"You saved me," Jack said.

BuZZZZZ

"I'm glad you're safe," Belle said. She flew high into the air. From this perspective she could see everything.

"I must find a home before dark," she said.

She flew until she saw a huge purple box. She landed and looked inside.

"This box looks like a safe place," Belle said. "I'll live here!"

She found a hole and crawled through it. The smell inside made Belle dizzy.

"I feel sick," she said.

"Belle! Come out! I smell poison!" Jack shouted.
Belle crawled out. She and Jack flew away.

"This time *you* saved *me*. Thanks!" Belle said.

Night would come soon, but Belle and Jack had
not found new homes.

"Jack?" Belle called over the wind. "I was wrong.
You are my friend. Let's look for a home together."

Jack laughed. "Sure!" They flew up high for a
better perspective of the area.

Yuk!

POISON

Belle saw green fields and a garden.

"Look, Jack!" Belle cried, flying down to land on a leaf. Jack sped after her and sat on a bright yellow flower.

"Welcome!" said a fuzzy caterpillar.

"I am looking for a new home," Belle said. "Can I live here?"

"Sure," the caterpillar said. "There is plenty of food here. We like ladybugs. You get rid of bugs that hurt garden plants."

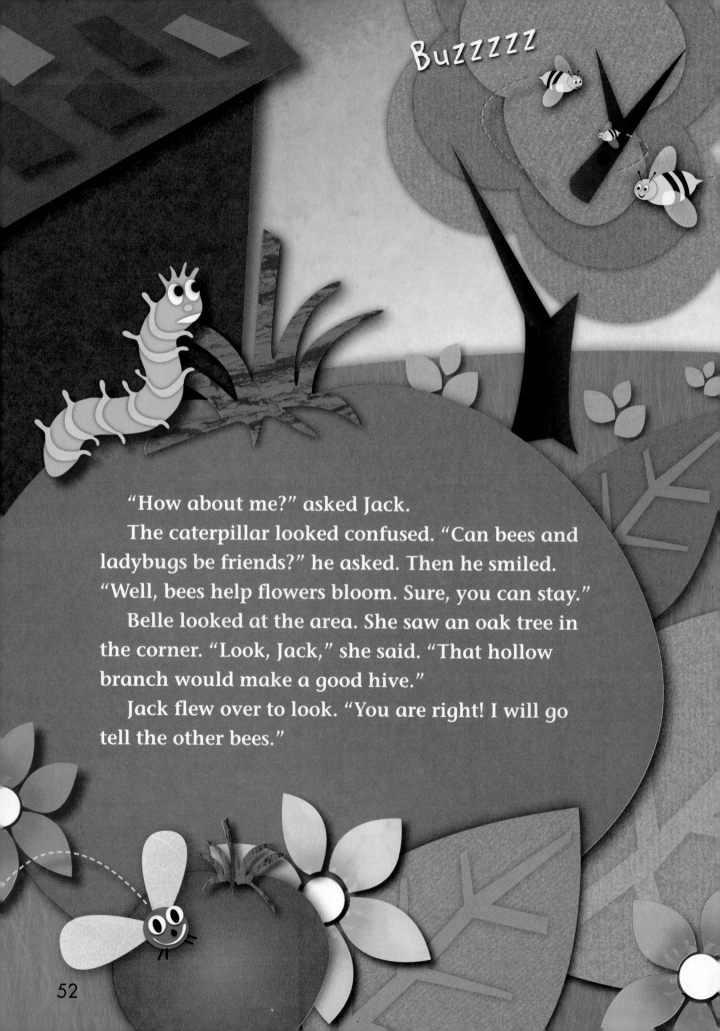

Buzzzzz

"How about me?" asked Jack.

The caterpillar looked confused. "Can bees and ladybugs be friends?" he asked. Then he smiled. "Well, bees help flowers bloom. Sure, you can stay."

Belle looked at the area. She saw an oak tree in the corner. "Look, Jack," she said. "That hollow branch would make a good hive."

Jack flew over to look. "You are right! I will go tell the other bees."

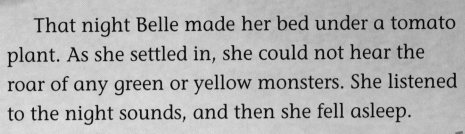

That night Belle made her bed under a tomato plant. As she settled in, she could not hear the roar of any green or yellow monsters. She listened to the night sounds, and then she fell asleep.

What Do You Think?

What is happening to the meadow where Belle and Jack first lived?

Aliens from Idaho!

TWO-EYED CREATURES COME TO MIDIA!

Strange creatures known as humans have landed on Midia.

The family of humans arrived in this territory sometime between the first and third sunset of this afternoon. They used a strange flying device for their long voyage.

These humans gave the Mayor of Midia red fluff they called "flowers." According to the Mayor, they were not very tasty.

"Don't be scared that we only have two eyes," said a tall human. "We come in peace."

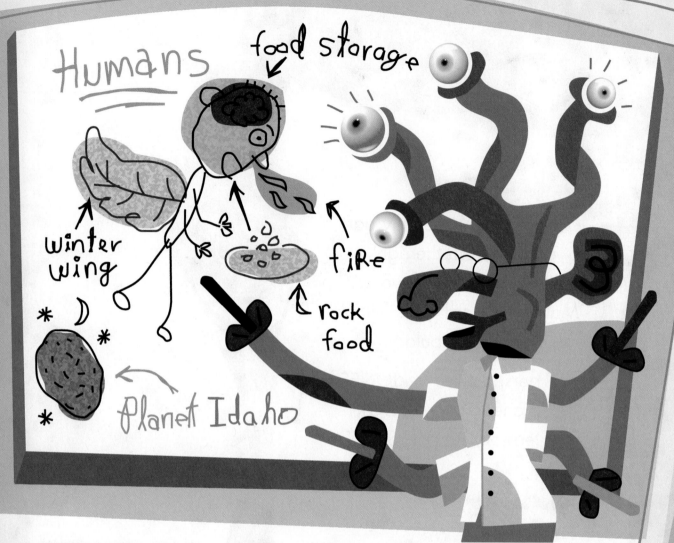

EXPERT EXPLAINS WHAT HUMANS ARE

Dr. Zweeb is a Midian scientist. He recently studied the aliens. He is a great expert on humans.

"Humans are very simple creatures," said the famous doctor. "They come from the planet Idaho," he stated. "They live underground and eat rocks. They store them in their bodies, behind their eyeballs. During winter, the humans grow their feathers and fly."

"But don't get them angry," warned Dr. Zweeb. "They just might blast fire through their noses!"

EXPLORATION

4 You 2 Do

Word Play

Explorers may see only part of an object. In the right column are parts of words. Match the word parts with this week's vocabulary.

perspective	IONEE
pioneers	ITORY
territory	SPECT

Making Connections

How are Belle and Jack like the doctors in the first selection?

On Paper

Which would you rather explore, how the human body works or deep space? Write a sentence that tells why you made your choice.

Contents

TRAVEL AMERICA

58

Words 2 the Wise

This week you'll read about **traveling America**. Think about how you would like to travel around the country.

Let's Explore

ROUTE US 66

Before 1938, there was no main road that connected Chicago to Los Angeles. Then Route 66 was built. It became "The Main Street of America." There was a popular song about it. There was also a television show. Route 66 was America's most famous highway.

Now people could drive from the Midwest to the West Coast. There were many unique places along the way. Travelers enjoyed the roadside attractions.

1. You can sleep in a concrete teepee at this motel.
2. Meteor City was a trading post built in 1938. They sold gifts that took you back in time.
3. These giant arrows are at an old, deserted truck stop.

There was the Iceberg Gas Station. It looked like a small mountain of snow. And there was the El Sombrero. This restaurant was shaped like a giant hat. Postcards of places like these also became popular.

By the 1970s, four-lane highways were built. People could travel faster now. They could also take planes. Soon, few people traveled the famous highway.

Today, many of the original Route 66 attractions still stand. There is even a Route 66 Museum.

A Cause for Walking

by Jamie McGillian

Walkers in California begin the first day of a three-day walk.

Can someone really walk across America? Many people have.

Some people walk to raise money for the American Cancer Society. First, they start by asking friends and family members for pledges. Pledges are promises to give money for each mile walked. Most people are happy to help. Some companies donate one dollar for each mile that a volunteer walks.

Eric Latham wanted to raise money for cancer research. He created the Walk About America program. His goal was to raise $50,000. He started walking on April 14, 2005. He began in North Carolina. He walked for 206 days. That is more than half a year! He finally crossed the Golden Gate Bridge in San Francisco. He was tired. But he was very proud. Congratulations, Eric!

Some people walk all the way across the country to raise money.

Eric Latham walked from North Carolina to California.

Volunteers meet amazing goals because they want to help others.

Volunteers get ready to run a race to raise money for cancer research.

Sometimes groups walk together. Hospital workers in West Virginia did this. They raised $27,000. Some walkers are cancer survivors. Other walkers know someone who has cancer.

Many walks are less than 10 miles long. Some walks are longer. A walk in Santa Monica, California, covered 39 miles.

Every year, the Susan G. Komen Breast Cancer Foundation organizes walks. These walks cover 60 miles in three days.

Twelve cities in the U.S. hold three-day walks. There are other walks in many cities in the U.S. Is there one near you?

Ron Reschke's friend died of cancer. He wants people with cancer to receive better treatments. He was willing to do a long walk for a cure. He set a goal to walk more than 1,000 miles!

Ron began his walk from Madison, the capital of Wisconsin.

A volunteer must train before trying to walk for three days.

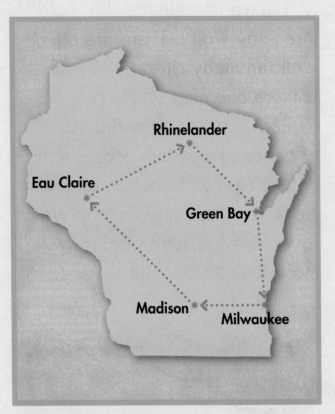

Ron Reschke walked around the state of Wisconsin to raise money.

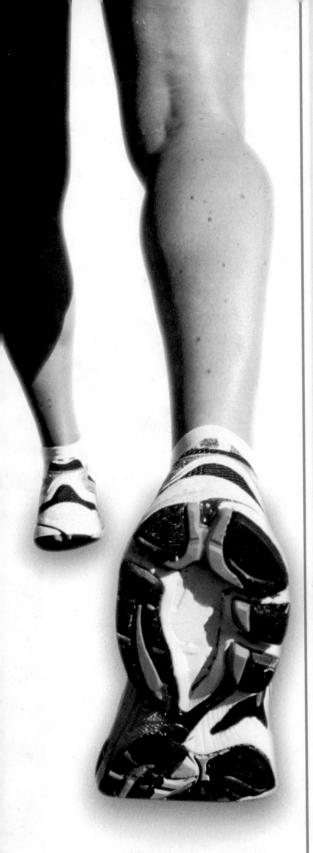

Supporters watched for Ron as he walked his route.

Ron walked across the state of Wisconsin. He walked for two and a half months. Ron stopped in ten cities. He visited hundreds of small towns. Ron walked 1,106 miles!

Ron did not use modern transportation. He went from place to place on foot. Some people followed Ron. Some walked. Some used other forms of transportation.

This walk helped Ron honor his friend. The money he raised will help cancer patients someday.

How do volunteers plan walks across one state or many states? Before and during the challenge, they follow this advice.

1 — Start training. Prepare your body. Start a regular exercise routine.

2 — Choose the right walking shoes.

3 — Get enough sleep. Drink plenty of water.

4 — Enjoy the scenery! Notice how the route changes during the walk.

Find out if there is a walk for a cause near your town.

During the walk, it's important to get plenty of rest.

5— Keep a journal. Write about the landmarks along the route. List the places you visit. Write about yourself. Do you have blisters on your feet? How many miles have you walked?

6— Bring a camera. Take pictures of people and places along your route. Create a scrapbook or slideshow of your travels.

Maybe you are not ready for a cross-country walk. Try a local walk. Remember to focus on the goal. It may get tough. But remember the cause. Your goal is the finish line. You can help millions!

What Do You Think?

What are three things someone needs to do before participating in a walk?

With proper training, you can reach your goal... the finish line!

The Longest Route

by
Dimitri Koval

illustrated by
Matt Phillips

The three cousins sat around the campfire. It was late at night. Their parents were in their cabins. Their younger brothers and sisters were all fast asleep.

The conversation soon turned to who had traveled the farthest to the Miller family reunion. Each year the reunion was held at a different place. It was in Florida last year. This year the Millers met in Colorado.

The cousins all lived in different parts of the United States. Kayla lived in Alabama. Sam lived in California. Janet lived in Kansas. Each family's journey used a different mode of transportation. The cousins shared their itineraries.

Kayla came by plane.

"I had to wake up at four in the morning! I was so tired," she complained.

Her first flight went from Alabama to Texas. It took almost two hours. Then she flew from Texas to Colorado.

"I just love flying," she said. "I had a window seat on both flights. The Earth is beautiful from high up in the sky. It looks like a giant quilt. Cars look like ants!"

The flight attendant had given Kayla a set of headphones. She listened to music.

"The only bad part was that my ears got plugged," she said. "I had to chew gum to help clear my ears."

Kayla finally arrived in Colorado at noon. It took only six hours.

"That's nothing. Our trip lasted for over a day!" Sam said. "We took a train from San Diego to Los Angeles. Then we took the train from Los Angeles to New Mexico. This took twenty-one hours. It took another four hours on a bus to get from New Mexico to Colorado."

Sam left at three in the afternoon on Friday. He arrived in Colorado at 5:30 in the afternoon the next day! The train makes many stops along the way.

"I really liked the train," Sam said. "We went through lots of small towns. I saw some old train stations too. The route that the train takes is really cool. It travels through mountains. And it travels through valleys. It travels through deserts. The views are amazing!"

Sam liked walking from car to car. And the conductors taught him a lot about the places they saw. His journey took over twenty-six hours!

Janet came by bus.

"I met lots of nice people," she said. "You have a lot of time to talk to people when you ride the bus."

She left Kansas at 6:30 in the morning. She arrived in Colorado at 8:45 that night.

"I had a window seat too," Janet said. "The views were great!"

She liked when the bus climbed the steep mountain roads. The bus also had small televisions. She watched a few movies. It took over fifteen hours to get to Colorado.

The cousins all agreed. Sam had the longest travel time. But Kayla traveled farthest and fastest. It is over 1,500 miles from Alabama to Colorado. That is four hundred miles more than Sam's journey.

They all said they loved traveling. It didn't matter if it was by plane, train, or bus. And it also didn't matter if they had long or short itineraries. Traveling gave them the opportunity to see the country.

As the moon sank below the treetops, there was only one competition left—who could stay up the longest!

What Do You Think?

In what order did the cousins arrive at the campsite in Colorado?

ODD PLACES, U.S.A.

These are not the usual places that tourists visit. Which one would you like to take a trip to see?

NEW JERSEY
LUCY THE ELEPHANT

Margate, New Jersey, is the only place you will see an elephant that is six stories high and weighs 90 tons. Lucy the Elephant was built in 1881. Lucy is made from a million pieces of wood. By the 1960s, she was in poor shape. A "Save Lucy" fund raised half a million dollars. Now, Lucy looks as good as new.

Spoonbridge and Cherry, 1988,
Claes Oldenburg and Coosje van Bruggen

MINNEAPOLIS

SPOONBRIDGE AND CHERRY

Have you ever seen a 1,500-pound cherry? The Minneapolis Sculpture Garden in Minnesota has the Spoonbridge and Cherry sculpture. The spoon weighs over 5,800 pounds! The sculpture crosses over a pond in a beautifully landscaped garden. This was all created for the sculpture. The sculpture is also a fountain. Water pours from the cherry's stem. This makes the cherry look shiny. Who wants a sundae?

FRONT DOOR, FRONT PAGE

In Rockport, Massachusetts, there is a house made entirely of newspaper. It took Elis Stenman twenty years to build it. The walls and the furniture are made of rolled newspaper. Home, sweet home!

ORLANDO

THE UPSIDE DOWN HOUSE

If you happen to find yourself in Orlando, Florida, you can't miss the upside down house. They say that the building was first located on an island. A huge tornado carried it hundreds of miles. It landed upside down on top of another building. It's a good story! But it's not true! The building is called Wonder Works. It was really built in 1998. Inside it is filled with lots of fun things to see and do.

4 You 2 Do

Word Play

Use a concept word to answer each riddle.

mile   mode   route

I'm a method of transportation. I am a _____.

I'm like a road. I am a _____.

I'm a unit of measure. I am a _____.

Use a concept word to create your own riddle!

Making Connections

The cousins in "The Longest Route" shared travel stories at the reunion. When volunteers meet on a walk, how do you think they pass the time?

On Paper

Write a postcard from a place you have visited or a place you would like to visit. Include the sights and sounds of this place. Tell why you are there.

SAN FRANCISCO

Answers for Word Play: mode, route, mile.

The Southwest

Contents

The Southwest

Choose an activity and explore this week's concept, the Southwest!

Words 2 the Wise

The Southwest has some beautiful and surprising scenery. As you read, think about what you know about the Southwest.

Let's Explore

SCENES FROM THE
SOUTHWEST

What do you know about the Southwest? Do you think it is just a desert? Some parts are arid and sandy. And it is the driest part of the United States. But it also has many other surprises.

You can ski down snow-capped mountains. You can hike down deep canyon trails. You can even raft down raging rivers. The Southwest is more than just a desert.

1. Sonoran Desert scene with saguaro cactus

2. The Colorado River slowly carved out the Grand Canyon over millions of years. This beautiful canyon attracts visitors from all over the world.

1

People who live in the Southwest have a rich history. Native Americans first learned to survive in the Southwest. They lived in its canyons and cliffs long ago.

Towns grew over time. Cowboys herded cattle. Miners searched for gold. Farmers grew what they could in the hot climate. Towns became large cities.

Many towns also died out. Ghost towns and ancient ruins are all that remain.

1. Cliff dwellings of Mesa Verde

2. Spanish settlers from Mexico brought ranching to the Southwest in the 1700s. This is how the cowboy way of life began here.

3. The skyline of Phoenix, Arizona. Phoenix is one of the fastest growing cities in the United States.

Wild, Wild Westerns

BY ETHAN BENMAR

The Southwest is full of beautiful landforms. Many look like red rock towers and cliffs. They rise above the arid desert plain. The landforms are called mesas and buttes. Wind and water carved them over time. Have you ever seen these unusual cliffs in movies? Hollywood filmed many westerns in the Southwest. Its landscape made a stunning background.

Early Westerns

People have always loved movies set in the West. They loved the scenes of the wild frontier. They watched sheriffs fighting outlaws. They saw cowboys ride off into the sunset.

These frontier settings were not real. Filmmakers shot the movies in movie studios. They painted all the scenes for the movies. They were shot quickly. And the costs were low.

Actors in early western movies acted in front of painted scenery.

On Location

Westerns started looking more realistic in the 1930s. The cameras improved. Filmmakers spent more money. They made longer movies. And they began filming scenes outdoors. John Ford was one of these directors. He changed westerns forever.

John Ford loved the desert. The landforms in Monument Valley, Arizona, were his favorite. It was arid. But it was also stunning. It would be the perfect setting for his next western.

Left: John Ford on location during the filming of the movie *Stagecoach*

Below: Monument Valley was the setting for John Ford's movie *Stagecoach*.

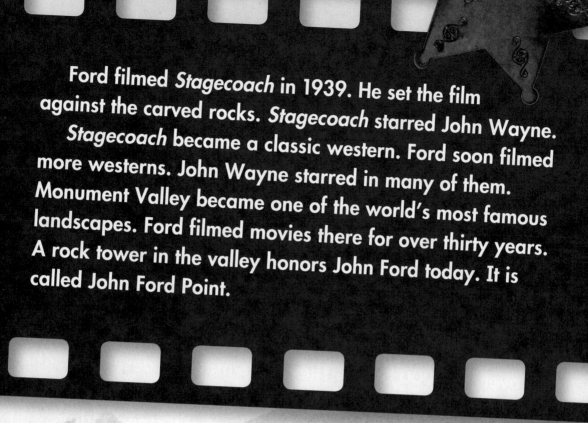

Ford filmed *Stagecoach* in 1939. He set the film against the carved rocks. *Stagecoach* starred John Wayne. *Stagecoach* became a classic western. Ford soon filmed more westerns. John Wayne starred in many of them. Monument Valley became one of the world's most famous landscapes. Ford filmed movies there for over thirty years. A rock tower in the valley honors John Ford today. It is called John Ford Point.

Actor John Wayne (left) and director John Ford (right) on location for a movie

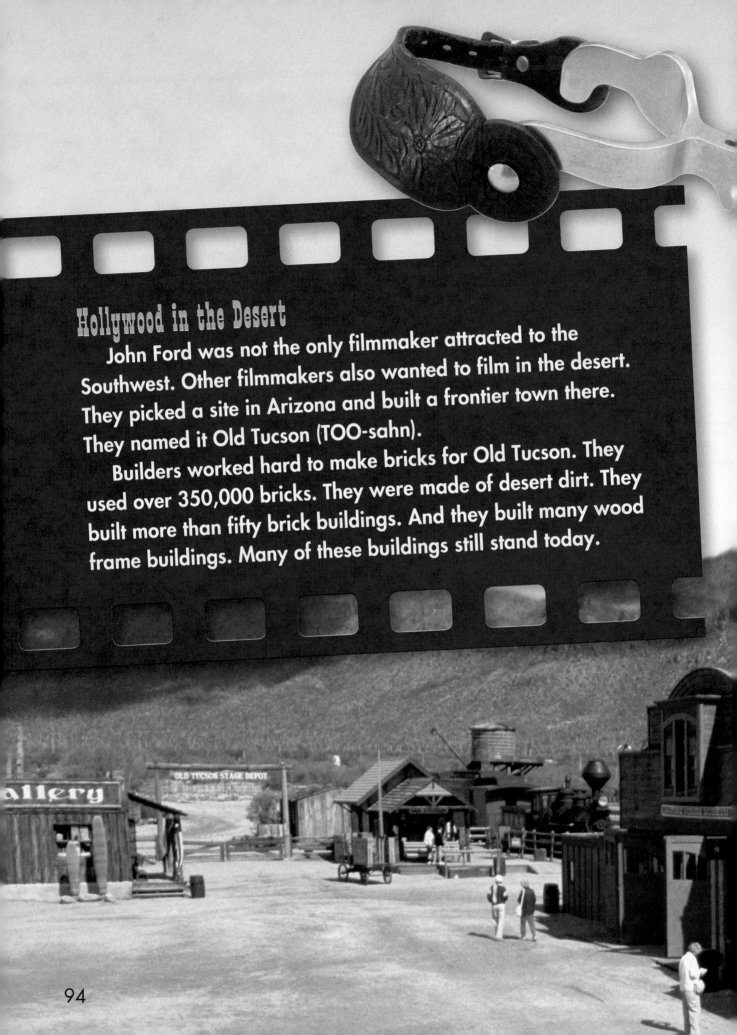

Hollywood in the Desert

John Ford was not the only filmmaker attracted to the Southwest. Other filmmakers also wanted to film in the desert. They picked a site in Arizona and built a frontier town there. They named it Old Tucson (TOO-sahn).

Builders worked hard to make bricks for Old Tucson. They used over 350,000 bricks. They were made of desert dirt. They built more than fifty brick buildings. And they built many wood frame buildings. Many of these buildings still stand today.

Arizona was the first movie filmed at Old Tucson. Many other films followed.

People kept going to westerns. Old Tucson grew with each new film. Builders added a saloon, a bank, and a doctor's office for one movie. Then they added a hotel. Then a jail and a ranch were built. Each new movie needed a different setting. Builders created them all. They even added a creek!

Old Tucson is a copy of an 1860s frontier town.

Old Tucson opened to the public in 1960. Visitors loved it. They could see where their favorite movies were made. They could watch actors perform stunts. And they could have their pictures taken in front of some famous settings.

Old Tucson also saw plenty of action in the 1970s. It was home to some TV shows too. One of the best known was "Little House on the Prairie."

A fire swept through Old Tucson in 1995. The fire destroyed many buildings. But Old Tucson was rebuilt in 1998. It still holds the title of "Hollywood in the Desert."

"Little House on the Prairie" was about an 1800s family. It was filmed at Old Tucson.

Old western movies filmed in the Southwest gave people ideas about the Wild West. Outlaws shot up peaceful towns. Steer roamed the land. Guitar-strumming cowboys herded cattle. And the red rock mountains stood tall in the background. It was a place of adventure. People from all over the world wanted to travel there.

Monument Valley gave westerns a stunning landscape. Old Tucson gave westerns a "real" frontier look. Both locations show the beauty of the Southwest.

What Do You Think?

In what ways were early westerns different from later westerns that were made?

SEARCHING FOR SURE FOOT

by Tamera Bryant   illustrated by Tom Newsom

Sarah pulled the old picture from her pocket. It showed a young girl standing on a big rock next to a pool of water. She was about ten years old, the same as Sarah. But the picture was taken in the Grand Canyon many years ago. The girl was Sarah's great-grandmother.

Sarah remembered her mother's words about Great-grandmother and her family. *Her tribe was known as "people of the blue-green water."*

Mom turned into the parking lot. *Finally!* They had been driving for two days. Sarah couldn't wait to get to the canyon trail.

Sarah stood at the edge of the canyon. *I might be standing where Great-grandmother stood once,* thought Sarah.

"Let's hike!" said Dad.

"Which way?" Sarah asked.

Mom and Dad both pointed down. Sarah laughed. She knew all about hiking. Steep trails didn't scare her. Besides, something special waited at the trail's end.

The hike took many hours. Everyone was tired when they reached the village of Supai (soo-PYE). The village had no mall or movie theater. Their room at the lodge had no television. *What did Great-grandmother do here?* wondered Sarah as she fell asleep.

The next morning, Sarah visited the store. She showed the old picture of her great-grandmother to the woman behind the counter. "Do you know where this picture was taken?" Sarah asked.

The woman gently took the picture. "Where did this come from?" she asked.

"From my mother," Sarah said. "The girl is my great-grandmother. She lived here a long time ago."

"Wait here," the woman said.

In a few minutes, the woman came back. She was with the oldest person Sarah had ever seen. "I think Mr. Manakaja (Mahn-ah-KAH-jah) here can help you," she said.

"Did you know my great-grandmother?" Sarah asked the old man.

"Yes, I did," he said softly. "She left in the 1950s."

"What was she like?" Sarah asked.

"We called her Sure Foot. She could go anywhere in the canyon without falling." Mr. Manakaja smiled. "This picture was taken at the bottom of Mooney Falls. If you go there, you'll know how Sure Foot got her name."

Sarah and her parents hired a guide to take them to Mooney Falls. The guide said the hike down was rough.

Everyone started down slowly. The guide led the way. They held onto rough chains attached to the canyon walls and used safety ropes, too. For Sarah, every step along the trail was thrilling and frightening! Hiking had never been this scary.

A few minutes into the hike, Sarah slipped.
Her father caught her. Her heart pounded against
the picture in her shirt pocket. Great-grandmother
was sure-footed. She could be too.

The group passed through a tunnel. Just beyond,
Sarah spotted the blue-green pool of water. She ran to
its edge, enjoying the roar of the falls. She saw the big
rock right away. She climbed right on top.

Sarah's mother took a picture of her. Did she look as happy as Great-grandmother? She sure felt that way.

The next morning, Sarah saw Mr. Manakaja sitting in front of the store. She took the camera and walked over to him. Sarah clicked back to the picture of her on the big rock. As he looked at it, she whispered, "Thank you, Mr. Manakaja."

"You are welcome, Little Sure Foot," he said with a wink.

WHAT DO YOU THINK?

How do you think Sarah's climb down to the falls is different from her great-grandmother's climb? How might it be the same?

Desert Snow

by Pat Mora

Coyote spies
new moon, slight
grin, high
in the sky.

Coyote licks
cold, white
shine, mouthful
of stars.

Coyote serenades
Moon, grinning slyly
at hills sleeping in starry blankets,
at music rising, "Halloooooooooo!"

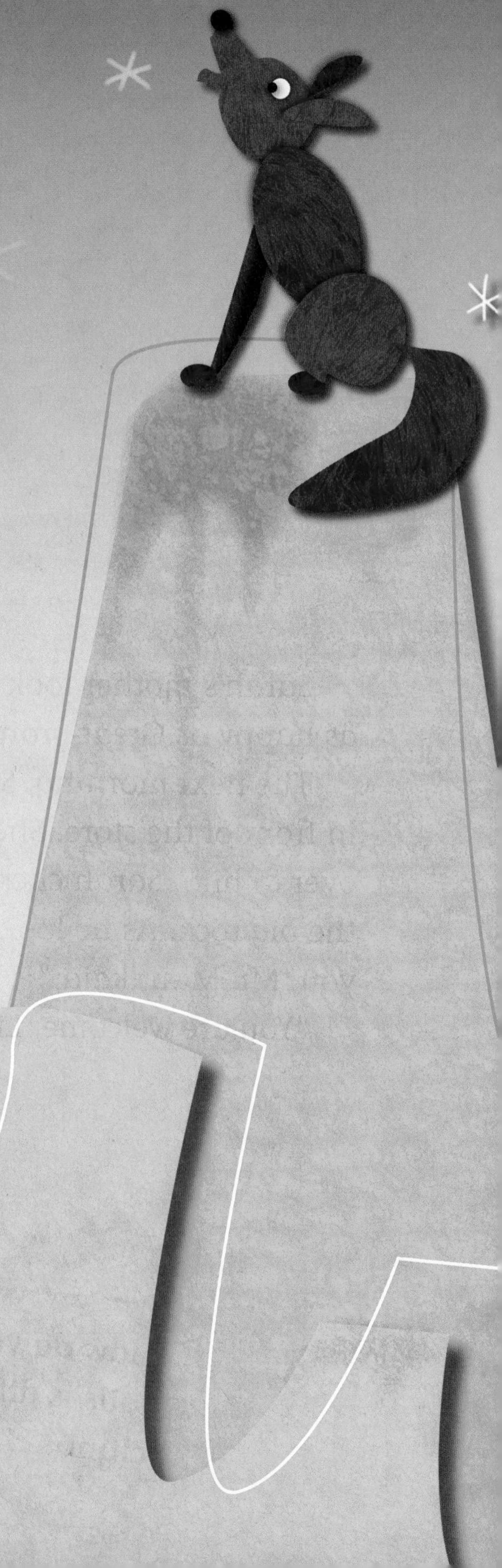

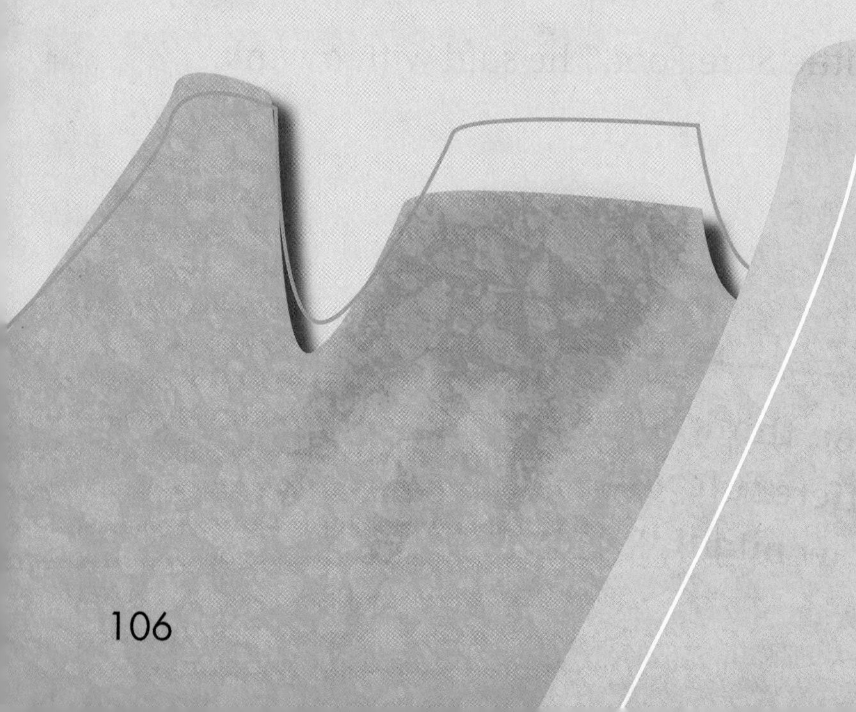

How The Maricopas Made Wishes Come True

by Byrd Baylor

They used to climb to a windy cave
up in the Painted Rock Mountains.

It was a place where any wish
was granted.

You had to go alone.
You had to creep
through a small dark hole
and sit there facing the light.
You had to hold your right hand out
and think of what you wanted.

It could be anything–
good crops or turquoise
or luck in racing
or someone to love.

The Maricopas are a Native
American people who live in
south-central Arizona.

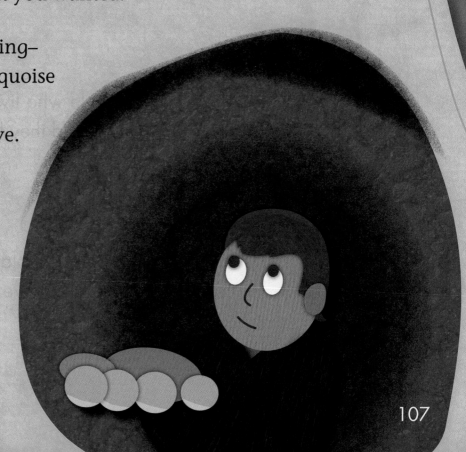

4 for 2 Do

Word Play

Play a guessing game with each of this week's concept vocabulary words. Don't say the word aloud. Instead, choose one of these ways to give hints.

- tell what it is not
- tell what it means
- give examples or act it out

Then let others guess the word.

frontier, arid, canyon, cliffs, carved, hiking, guide

Making Connections

This week you read about people who live and work in the Southwest. How did they learn about the land and its people?

On Paper

Think about an interesting or beautiful place in the Southwest or another place you have seen. Write about it.

the WEST

Contents

the WEST

Let's Explore

Words 2 the Wise

Do you think the **West** is the best? As you read, think about what you know about the western United States.

Paul Bunyan and Babe the Blue Ox stand tall at a spot called Trees of Mystery. The giant redwood trees around them are up to 4,000 years old!

CALIFORNIA

Looking for some unusual vacation photos? Then visit California! California is filled with beautiful sights. But it is also home to some very BIG attractions.

California has some of the world's biggest trees. People have carved some amazing statues out of the giant redwoods. There is a Paul Bunyan statue. It is 49 feet tall! Then there is a house carved from a single log.

The One-Log House has a kitchen, bedroom, living room, and dining room. It also has electric lights, two doors, two windows, and wheels!

There is also a gift shop made from a tree trunk. In California you can drive your car through a tree!

California is also home to some very big murals. The most famous is the whale mural. It is in Long Beach. It took over 7,000 gallons of paint! At one time it was the world's largest mural. California has lots of BIG surprises. Get your camera ready!

This gift shop sits inside a giant redwood tree trunk! The trunk is about 2,500 years old.

For years, the whale mural was the world's biggest mural, or wall painting.

Surf's

by Liese Vogel

For many people in California, surfing is a way of life!

California has over 1,000 miles of shoreline. Much of that is beach. Many of these beaches are great for surfing. The waves are wild in northern California. But they are easier to ride in southern California. The weather on the coast is mild to hot. People can surf all year.

up!

Above: George Freeth introduced surfing to California in the early 1900s.

George Freeth first brought surfing to California. He demonstrated the sport in 1907. He attracted big crowds. People wanted to see the man who could "walk on water." He was astonishing. George was a champion surfer from Hawaii. The sport had been popular in Hawaii for at least 1,000 years.

The man above is surfing in a pool designed to form waves.

Surfing became very popular in California in the 1950s. Now it is popular around the world. Some people earn money from surfing. They enter surfing contests. Their skills are unbelievable! There are even surfing magazines and videos.

People don't need much gear to surf. And they can surf wherever waves form naturally. Waves form on oceans. Waves form on lakes and rivers. People can even surf in pools designed to form waves!

California has many top surfing spots. Many surfers travel there. They come from all over the world. Many of them head to Huntington Beach. It is known as "Surf City." Huntington is an unbroken stretch of beach. It is more than eight miles long. The waves are always good. There are surfing contests there. Crowds watch the pros. The surfers do astonishing moves out on the waves. It is unbelievable!

Huntington Beach, California, is a popular destination for surfers from around the world.

Surfers have their own language. Your board is a "stick." You "get mullered" when you wipe out. You're "stoked" when you are excited. A wave is not just a wave to surfers. They call waves "swells." A "barreling" wave is one that is long and hollow. It looks like a tube. A barrel is the ultimate wave. A "pipeline" is where all the waves are barreling. It is one of the most famous waves. It is also one of the most photographed waves.

Surfing a pipeline is very difficult.

Members of Surfers Against Sewage (SAS) want everyone, not just surfers, to have clean water.

SURFERS AGAINST SEWAGE

SURFERS SEW AGAINST TOXIC WASTE

Barrels and pipelines aren't the only problems surfers face. The water itself may be a problem. It may be polluted. Many surfers are concerned about polluted water. A group of surfers formed Surfers Against Sewage (SAS) in 1990. Sewage is waste from buildings and houses. It is carried through sewers. The SAS works to prevent sewage from being put in the ocean. They want everyone to enjoy the water.

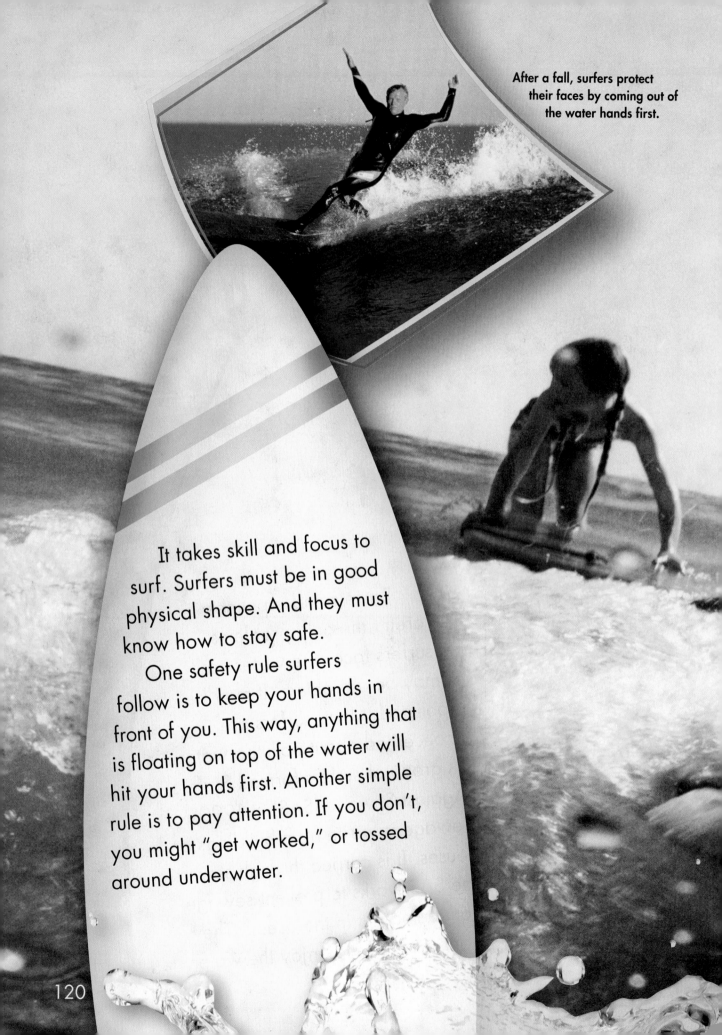

After a fall, surfers protect their faces by coming out of the water hands first.

It takes skill and focus to surf. Surfers must be in good physical shape. And they must know how to stay safe.

One safety rule surfers follow is to keep your hands in front of you. This way, anything that is floating on top of the water will hit your hands first. Another simple rule is to pay attention. If you don't, you might "get worked," or tossed around underwater.

You don't have to be from California to learn how to surf. It is possible to learn to surf on any shoreline. Or you can surf wherever there are waves. You need the right equipment. You need the right conditions. And you need an experienced teacher.

California and surfing go together naturally. Chances are, someone is heading down to the beach with a board right now.

Surf's up!

Skateboarding, also known as sidewalk surfing, started in California in the 1950s. Surfers began building skateboards to surf the streets.

What Do You Think?

Why is surfing so popular in California?

NATURAL TREASURES

by Lillian Vance

Would you protect your treasures? Our nation does. Read about these natural treasures!

Alaska

Denali National Park

Mount McKinley is the tallest mountain in North America. It is 20,320 feet high! It is in Denali (Duh-NAHL-ee) National Park. Visitors to the park can explore forests. And they can see gigantic sheets of ice. They are called glaciers (GLAY-shurz). Dall sheep live here. Grizzly bears live here. And moose live here. It is very cold.

California

Death Valley National Park

Death Valley is the lowest point in North America. It is 282 feet below sea level. It is also one of the hottest places on Earth. The temperature reached 134° F on July 10, 1913. That is the hottest temperature ever recorded in the United States!

In 1849, miners on their way to the California Gold Rush named the valley.

California

Yosemite National Park

Yosemite (yoh-SEHM-ih-tee) Valley looks like a gigantic "U." Its rocky cliffs scrape the sky. Huge waterfalls spill over the cliffs. And sequoia (si-KWOY-uh) trees stand like giants. They are the largest living trees in the world! Black bears roam freely. Bighorn sheep also roam freely. Visitors love Yosemite. It is one of our most beautiful parks.

Idaho
Montana
Wyoming

Yellowstone National Park

Yellowstone is America's oldest national park. Volcanic eruptions and freezing ice shaped Yellowstone. They squeezed and scraped the land. They formed valleys. They pushed up mountains. And they formed huge lakes.

The ground below Yellowstone is still hot. Gas and steam bubble up from many spots underground. Researchers predict another volcano will erupt in the future. Yellowstone is a unique park! It is a top spot for visitors.

California

Joshua Tree National Park

This national park can seem brutal and unwelcoming. Strong winds, rain, and extreme climates shaped this desert landscape. The Colorado Desert and the Mojave (moh-HAH-vee) Desert join in this national park.

This park is named after its slow-growing trees. Joshua trees grow about one-half inch per year. These trees can live about two hundred years. The tallest Joshua tree is forty feet high. It is over 300 years old!

Oregon

Crater Lake National Park

Crater Lake is the deepest lake in America. It is 1,932 feet deep! A volcanic eruption formed it. The eruption made a gigantic hole. The hole is called a crater. Forests dot the cliffs above the lake. Most lakes have streams flowing into or out of them, but Crater Lake does not. For this reason, the water is crystal clear and has an eye-catching blue color. Over half a million people visit Crater Lake each year.

Utah

Arches National Park

This park is famous for its unusual rock formations. Visitors walk under curving arches. The arches are huge. The park has over 2,000 natural arches. Delicate Arch is the most famous arch. People can stand beside rocky towers. Some towers have rocks that balance on top. It is a quiet place during the day. But at night the animals come out to hunt. Lizards and mule deer roam the land.

Washington

Olympic National Park

Visitors can experience three climates in this park. One is the coast. It has rocky beaches. The beaches are foggy. Another climate is the mountain area. These mountains are covered with snow and glaciers. And there is the rain forest. It is not a tropical rain forest. But it is just as wet. Up to fourteen feet of rain falls here every year!

WHAT DO YOU THINK?

Which park would you like to visit? Why?

All Steamed Up

The geyser (GY-zuhr) is ready to erupt! This one is named Old Faithful. It's the most famous geyser at Yellowstone National Park. Geysers are rare. Only about 1,000 exist worldwide. Over half are at Yellowstone. Let's watch!

Old Faithful gets its name from the fact that it erupts at least once every few hours.

You know it's coming when the ground starts to rumble and shake. Next, you hear gurgling noises. Then it happens. Thousands of gallons of boiling water explode from underground. Water sprays high into the sky. A huge steam cloud fills the air. This lasts a few minutes. Then the show's over. In an hour or so, it will start all over again.

Visitors watch safely from more than 300 feet away. The geyser sprays 90 to 180 feet into the air.

Geyser

1

Hot Spring

2

What causes these eruptions? Centuries ago, a volcano stood where Yellowstone National Park is today. A huge eruption blew the volcano apart. Hot, liquid rock runs deep underground. It heats the rock layers nearby.

Surface water trickles underground. The water heats up as it passes through the hot rock layers. Then it starts to rise back up. The hot water becomes trapped in the tight spaces.

The water begins to steam and bubble. The hot water has nowhere to go. That makes pressure! The pressure pushes the water up. And boiling water shoots out of the top of a geyser!

Soon it will start over again. That's why this geyser is called Old Faithful.

Mudpot

③

④

Fumarole

(1) A geyser shoots hot water into the air.

(2) A hot spring is a pool of heated water.

(3) A hot mudpot in the Solfatara field.

(4) A fumarole (FYOO-mah-roll) is like a vent. It releases hot steam.

4 you 2 Do

Word Play

What place do you know that you think is unbelievable? List words to describe that place. Use this week's concept vocabulary words or other words you know.

Making Connections

Why is it important to protect our national parks and environment? What are some ways you can help protect the environment in your community?

On Paper

Imagine you are at one of the places you read about. Write a postcard describing it. Add a drawing to the postcard.

Answers for Word Play: Answers will vary but words can include unbelievable, astonishing, indescribable, gigantic, amazing, incredible, enormous, fantastic, unreal.

Glossary

ar·e·a (âr′ ē ə), *NOUN.* 1. the amount of space something covers: *A large area of the earth is covered by water.* 2. a place: *The playground area is right outside.*

ar·id (ar′ id), *ADJECTIVE.* having very little rainfall; dry: *Deserts in Arizona are arid.*

as·ton·ish (ə ston′ ish), *VERB.* to surprise greatly; amaze: *I was astonished by the animals in the zoo.* **as·ton·ish·ed, as·ton·ish·ing.**

back·ground (bak′ ground′), *NOUN.* past experience, knowledge, and training: *A part of her background is that she has lived in the city.*

can·yon (kan′ yən), NOUN. a narrow valley with high, steep sides, usually with a stream at the bottom: *The Grand Canyon is a national park.*

carve (kärv), VERB. to cut something: *Statues can be carved out of stone.* **carved, carv·ing.**

cliff (klif), NOUN. a very steep, rocky slope: *It is a long drop off the edge of the cliff.*

con·fuse (kən fyüz′), VERB. to mix up; not to be sure about something: *Her directions confused me and I got lost.* **con·fused, con·fus·ing.**

a in hat	ō in open	sh in she
ā in age	ȯ in all	th in thin
â in care	ô in order	ŦH in then
ä in far	oi in oil	zh in measure
e in let	ou in out	ə = a in about
ē in equal	u in cup	ə = e in taken
ėr in term	u̇ in put	ə = i in pencil
i in it	ü in rule	ə = o in lemon
ī in ice	ch in child	ə = u in circus
o in hot	ng in long	

cul·ture (kul′ chər), *NOUN.*
a way of life, including foods,
celebrations, and languages:
*Each month we learn about
many different cultures.*

de·vice (di vis′), *NOUN.* something invented for use:
*Doctors use a device to help patients find out what is
wrong with them.*

e·rup·tion (i rup′ shən), *NOUN.*
an explosion of lava or steam
from a volcano: *The eruption
of the volcano was amazing
to see.*

eth·nic (eth′ nik), *ADJECTIVE.* a group of people of the same
race, nationality, and culture: *There are many different
ethnic groups in large cities.*

form (fôrm), *VERB*. 1. to take shape: *Clouds form in the sky.*
2. to become: *Water forms ice when it freezes.*
formed, form·ing.

fron·tier (frun tir′), *NOUN*. the farthest edge of settled country,
where the wilderness begins: *Many pioneers traveled
West to live on the open frontier.*

gi·gan·tic (jī gan′ tik), *ADJECTIVE*. like a giant; very large or
powerful; huge: *The redwood trees are gigantic.*

guide (gīd), *NOUN*. someone
or something that shows
the way: *We followed the
tour guide through the trails.*

a in hat	ō in open	sh in she
ā in age	ȯ in all	th in thin
â in care	ô in order	ŦH in then
ä in far	oi in oil	zh in measure
e in let	ou in out	ə = a in about
ē in equal	u in cup	ə = e in taken
ėr in term	u̇ in put	ə = i in pencil
i in it	ü in rule	ə = o in lemon
ī in ice	ch in child	ə = u in circus
o in hot	ng in long	

hike (hīk), 1. *VERB.* to take a long walk; march: *I hiked to the lake this morning.* 2. *NOUN.* a long walk; a march: *It was a four-mile hike through the forest to the camp.* *VERB* **hiked, hik·ing.**

home·sick (hōm′ sik′), *ADJECTIVE.* very sad because you are far away from home: *When I was in Europe, I was homesick.*

i·tin·e·rar·y (ī′ tin ə rer ē), *NOUN.* 1. route of travel; plan of travel: *I need to look at my itinerary for today.* 2. guidebook for travelers: *Many itineraries include a dress code.* *PL.* **i·tin·e·rar·ies.**

jour·ney (jer′ nē), 1. *NOUN.* a long trip from one place to another: *She took a journey across the United States.* 2. *VERB.* to travel; take a trip: *He journeyed South during the winter.* *VERB* **jour·neyed, jour·ney·ing.**

mile (mīl), *NOUN.* a unit for measuring length or distance: *I walked five miles today.*

mode (mōd), *NOUN.* the way or manner in which something is done; method: *Riding a car is a slower mode of transportation than riding in a plane.*

nat·ur·al·ly (nach′ ər ə lē), *ADVERB.* in a natural way: *Speak naturally; don't try to imitate someone else.*

per·spec·tive (pər spek′ tiv), *NOUN.* the view of something from a distance: *From my perspective I can see the sign clearly.*

a	in hat	ō	in open	sh	in she
ā	in age	ȯ	in all	th	in thin
â	in care	ô	in order	ŦH	in then
ä	in far	oi	in oil	zh	in measure
e	in let	ou	in out	ə	= a in about
ē	in equal	u	in cup	ə	= e in taken
ėr	in term	ů	in put	ə	= i in pencil
i	in it	ü	in rule	ə	= o in lemon
ī	in ice	ch	in child	ə	= u in circus
o	in hot	ng	in long		

pi·o·neer (pī′ ə nir′), NOUN. someone who goes first, or does something first, and so prepares a way for other people: *Elizabeth Blackwell was a pioneer in medicine.*

route (rüt *or* rout), NOUN. a way that you choose to get somewhere: *What route do you take to get to school?*

ter·ri·to·ry (ter′ ə tôr′ ē), NOUN. land; one of the parts of a country: *Much territory in the northern part of Africa is desert.* PL. **ter·ri·to·ries.**

trans·late (tran slát′), VERB. to change something from one language into another: *I translated the sentence from Spanish to English.* **trans·la·ted, trans·la·ting.**

trans·por·ta·tion (tran′ spər ta′ shən), NOUN. a way to move people or things: *When the bus broke down, we had no other transportation to school.*

un·be·liev·a·ble (un′ bi lē′ və bəl), ADJECTIVE. thinking something is not true: *The story was unbelievable.*

un·der·stand·ing (un′ der stan′ ding), NOUN. the act or fact of knowing something; knowledge: *She has a clear understanding of the problem.*

view (vyü), NOUN. 1. what you can see from a certain place: *My view of the canyon was amazing.* 2. the act of seeing; sight: *We saw different views of the island.* 3. the distance at which the eye can see something: *The airplane is in clear view.*

voy·age (voi′ ij), NOUN. a journey by water; cruise: *The sea was choppy on the voyage home.*

a in hat	ō in open	sh in she
ā in age	ȯ in all	th in thin
â in care	ô in order	ᴛʜ in then
ä in far	oi in oil	zh in measure
e in let	ou in out	ə = a in about
ē in equal	u in cup	ə = e in taken
ėr in term	u̇ in put	ə = i in pencil
i in it	ü in rule	ə = o in lemon
ī in ice	ch in child	ə = u in circus
o in hot	ng in long	

Acknowledgments

Text

Every effort has been made to locate the copyright owner of material reproduced in this component. Omissions brought to our attention will be corrected in subsequent editions. Grateful acknowledgment is made to the following for copyrighted material.

106 Curtis Brown, Ltd. "Desert Snow" by Pat Mora, first published in *This Big Sky* by Scholastic Press. Text copyright © 1998 by Pat Mora. Used by permission of Curtis Brown Ltd. All rights reserved.

107 Marian Reiner, Literary Agent "How the Maricopas Made Wishes Come True" by Byrd Baylor from *A God on Every Mountain Top*. Text copyright © 1981 by Byrd Baylor. Used by permission of Marian Reiner.

Illustrations

Cover: Laurie Keller; **20–26** Laurie Keller; **54** Mark Betcher; **70–77** Matt Phillips; **98–105** Tom Newsom.

Photographs

Every effort has been made to secure permission and provide appropriate credit for photographic material. The publisher deeply regrets any omission and pledges to correct errors called to its attention in subsequent editions.

Unless otherwise acknowledged, all photographs are the property of Pearson Education, Inc.

Photo locators denoted as follows: Top (T), Center (C), Bottom (B), Left (L), Right (R), Background (Bkgd)

Cover: (CL) ©Blasius Erlinger/Getty Images, (BL) Getty Images, (CR) ©Kelly-Mooney Photography/Corbis, (CR) ©Lew Robertson/Corbis, (CR) ©Mark A. Johnson/Corbis, (TL) ©Zigmund Leszczynski/Animals Animals/Earth Scenes; **1** (CL) Getty Images; **2** (T) Getty Images; **3** (R) Getty Images, (BR) ©Lew Robertson/Corbis, (TR) ©Robert Pickett/Corbis, (T) ©Uli Wiesmeier/zefa/Corbis; **5** (C) ©Purestock/Thinkstock; **6** (TR) ©Jason Lee/Reuters/Corbis; **7** (BR) Getty Images, (BL) ©Virgo/zefa/Corbis; **8** (BL) Getty Images, (R) ©Jason Lee/Reuters/Corbis; **9** (L) ©Richard Cummins/Corbis, (BR) Getty Images; **10** (R) ©David Forbert/SuperStock, (TC) Getty Images; **11** (BR) Getty Images, (L) ©Shannon Stapleton/Corbis; **12** (C) Mary Evans Picture Library; **13** (CR) ©Erich Lessing/Art Resource, NY, (R) Getty Images; **14** (TR) ©DK Images, (BL) ©Virgo/zefa/Corbis; **16** (C) ©Bob Krist/Corbis, (R) ©DK Images; **17** (R, C) Sylvain Leroux/Fula Flute Ensemble; **18** (R) Getty Images, (L) ©Michael St. Maur Sheil/Corbis; **19** (R, CL) ©DK Images, (CR) Sylvain Leroux/Fula Flute Ensemble; **31** (C) ©Grace/zefa/Corbis; **32** (TR) Getty Images; **33** (CL) Dave King/©DK Images, (BC) Getty Images, (CR) Cordelia Molloy/Photo Researchers, Inc.; **34** (C) Getty Images; **35** (TR) ©Inmagine/Alamy, (C) NASA; **36** Digital Vision/Thinkstock; **37** (C) M. I. Walker/Photo Researchers, Inc.; **38** (C) ©20TH Century Fox/The Kobal Collection; **39** (CR) ©Royalty-Free/Corbis; **40** (C) ©ALIX-IGR/Photo Researchers, Inc., (BL) Dave King/©DK Images; **41** (B) Cordelia Molloy/Photo Researchers, Inc.; **42** (CL, C) ©James King-Holmes/Photo Researchers, Inc.;

43 (C) ©James King-Holmes/Photo Researchers, Inc.; **44** (C) AP/Wide World Photos; **45** (CR) ©Science Photo Library/Superstock; **56** (R) Getty Images; **57** (C) ©Andrew Ballantyne; **59** (TCL, BR) Getty Images, (BL) ©Kelly-Mooney Photography/Corbis, (TL) ©Walter Bibikow/AGE Fotostock; **60** (C) ©Dick Reed/Corbis, (TC) Getty Images; **61** (CR, CL) ©Franck Fotos/Alamy Images, (TR) ©Walter Bibikow/AGE Fotostock; **62** (TL) ©Royalty-Free/Corbis, (TR) Getty Images, (TCR) ©Rod Rolle/Getty Images; **63** (CR) ©Eric Latham/Walk About America, (C) Getty Images; **64** (C) Angela Rowlings/AP/Wide World Photos; **65** (R) ©Royalty-Free/Corbis, (C) ©Richard Cummins/Corbis; **66** (L) ©Uli Wiesmeier/zefa/Corbis; **67** (BL, BC) Getty Images, (R) ©John Amis/AP/Wide World Photos; **68** (CC) ©Image Source/Getty Images, (BC) Stockdisc; **69** (T) ©Uli Wiesmeier/zefa/Corbis; **78** (BC) ©Kelly-Mooney Photography/Corbis; **79** (T) ©Garry Black/Masterfile Corporation; **80** (T) ©Lisa Poole/AP/Wide World Photos; **81** (B) ©Ian Dagnall/Alamy Images; **82** (BR) Getty Images; **83** (C) ©Ron Niebrugge/Alamy Images; **84** (TR, C) Getty Images; **85** (BC) ©Greg Probst/Corbis, (CL) ©Lightworks Media/Alamy Images; **86** (TR) ©Darrell Gulin/Corbis, (CR) ©George H. H. Huey/Corbis; **87** (BC) Getty Images, (R) ©Greg Probst/Corbis; **88** (BR) ©Royalty-Free/Corbis, (TR) Getty Images; **89** (CL) ©Design Pics/Index Open, (C) ©Jupiter Images, (T) ©Richard Cummins/AGE Fotostock; **90** (CL) Getty Images, (C) ©Richard Hamilton Smith/Corbis; **91** (BR) ©General Photographic Agency/Stringer/Getty Images; **92** (BR) Everett Collection, Inc., (CL) ©United Artists/The Kobal Collection; **93** (B) ©Bettmann/Corbis, (TR) Getty Images; **94** (B) ©Buddy Mays/Corbis, (TR) Getty Images; **95** (CR) ©Lightworks Media/Alamy Images; **96** (BR) ©Fotos International/Contributor/Getty Images, (CL) Geoff Brightling/©DK Images; **97** (BR) Getty Images, (C) ©Henryk T. Kaiser/Index Stock Imagery; **108** (TR) Stockdisc; **109** (C) ©David Trood/Getty Images; **111** (BL) ©Royalty-Free/Corbis, (BC) ©Blasius Erlinger/Getty Images, (BCL) ©Darrell Gulin/Corbis, (CL) ©Mark A. Johnson/Corbis; **112** (TR) ©LeighSmithImages/Alamy Images; **113** (CR) ©Jarl de Boer/The Tunneltree Archive, (BC) ©Robert Harding Picture Library Ltd/Alamy Images; **114** (L) ©Mark A. Johnson/Corbis; **115** (TR) ©The Surfing Museum, Ltd., (BL) ©Lew Robertson/Corbis; **116** (TC) ©PCL/Alamy Images, (C) ©Ron Brazil/ZUMA/Corbis; **117** (CR) ©Jeff Greenberg/AGE Fotostock; **118** (CL) ©Allsport Australia/ALLSPORT/Getty Images, (C) ©David Pu'u/Corbis; **119** (TR) ©Chinch Gryniewicz/Ecoscene/Corbis; **120** (TC) ©David Pu'u/Corbis, (C) ©Eric O'Connell/Getty Images; **121** (CL) ©FogStock/Index Open; **122** (CC) Digital Vision, (T) Getty Images; **123** (T) Brand X Pictures, (TR) Jupiter Images, (BL) ©Robert Pickett/Corbis; **124** (C, B) Getty Images; **125** (TR) ©Royalty-Free/Corbis, (C) Getty Images; **126** (C) Getty Images; **127** (C) Getty Images, (TR) Zigmund Leszczynski/Animals Animals/Earth Scenes; **128** (C, BR) Getty Images; **129** (C) Jupiter Images; **130** (C) ©Royalty-Free/Corbis; **131** (BL) ©Royalty-Free/Corbis; **132** (C) Brand X Pictures, (TL) ©Darrell Gulin/Corbis; **133** (C) ©Imagebroker/Alamy, (CR) Shutterstock; **134** (BR) ©Blasius Erlinger/Getty Images; **136** (C) Digital Vision, (TR) ©MedioImages/Getty Images; **137** (TC) Getty Images; **138** (TR, CR) Getty Images; **139** (CR) Getty Images; **140** (C) Getty Images; **141** (C) Getty Images; **142** (TR, BR) Getty Images; **143** (C) Getty Images.

MY SiDEWALKS ON
SCOTT FORESMAN
READING STREET

UNIT 1

PEARSON

Scott Foresman

pearsonschool.com

ISBN-13: 978-0-328-45286-6
ISBN-10:   0-328-45286-6

EAN

9 780328 452866

90000 >

Level D1